DISCOVERIES AROUND THE WORLD

GREAT MINDS AND FINDS IN
AUSTRALIA

Robin Koontz

A Division of

Before Reading: *Building Background Knowledge and Vocabulary*

Building background knowledge can help children process new information and build upon what they already know. Before reading a book, it is important to tap into what children already know about the topic. This will help them develop their vocabulary and increase their reading comprehension.

Questions and Activities to Build Background Knowledge:

1. Look at the front cover of the book and read the title. What do you think this book will be about?
2. What do you already know about this topic?
3. Take a book walk and skim the pages. Look at the table of contents, photographs, captions, and bold words. Did these text features give you any information or predictions about what you will read in this book?

Vocabulary: *Vocabulary Is Key to Reading Comprehension*

Use the following directions to prompt a conversation about each word.

- Read the vocabulary words.
- What comes to mind when you see each word?
- What do you think each word means?

> **Vocabulary Words:**
> - *Aboriginal*
> - *aircraft*
> - *architect*
> - *conservation*
> - *genetic*
> - *geological*
> - *hemisphere*
> - *Indigenous*
> - *meteorite*
> - *stromatolites*

During Reading: *Reading for Meaning and Understanding*

To achieve deep comprehension of a book, children are encouraged to use close reading strategies. During reading, it is important to have children stop and make connections. These connections result in deeper analysis and understanding of a book.

 Close Reading a Text

During reading, have children stop and talk about the following:

- Any confusing parts
- Any unknown words
- Text to text, text to self, text to world connections
- The main idea in each chapter or heading

Encourage children to use context clues to determine the meaning of any unknown words. These strategies will help children learn to analyze the text more thoroughly as they read.

When you are finished reading this book, turn to the next-to-last page for **Text-Dependent Questions** and an **Extension Activity**.

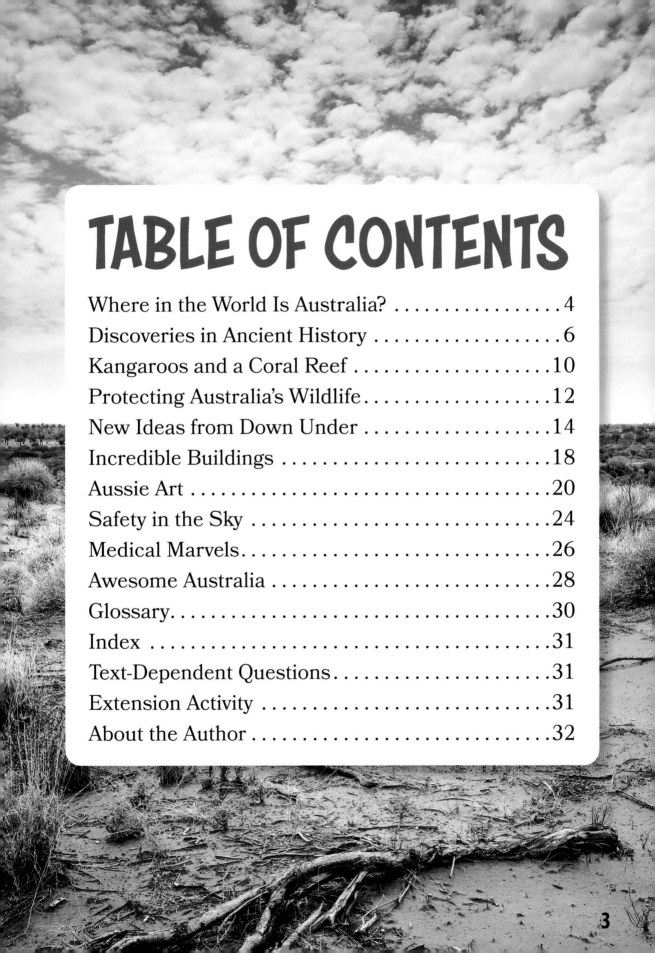

TABLE OF CONTENTS

WHERE IN THE WORLD IS AUSTRALIA?

The smallest of all of the continents, Australia is the only continent on Earth that is a single country. It is completely surrounded by water. Australia is divided into six states and two territories.

AUSTRALIA

What's in a Name?

"Aussie" is sometimes used to describe a person or thing from Australia. Some people call Australia itself "Oz."

Many Australians celebrate the national flag on September 3rd.

Australia is often called the "land down under" because it is in the southern **hemisphere**. About 80% of the people there live in the southeastern part of the country. Journey through Australia to discover its fascinating people and places. Find out what ideas and inventions come from this amazing part of the world.

Australia by the Numbers

 Population: >25.5 million

 Size: >2.9 million square miles or >7.7 million square kilometers

 Highest Point: Mount Kosciuszko, >7,310 feet or 2,228 meters

DISCOVERIES IN ANCIENT HISTORY

Some of the oldest **geological** features in the world are found in Australia. A 2,700-million-year-old section of rock there is called Wave Rock.

The colorful streaks in Wave Rock were made when rain caused chemicals from Earth to wash over the rock.

Uluru appears to change color throughout the day and year. It looks more red at dawn and at sunset.

The boulders of Karlu Karlu are made of granite and were formed over millions of years.

Karlu Karlu is the name for both an area and the rocks inside it. There, boulders balance on top of one another like large marbles. Uluru, a gigantic piece of sandstone, was formed 550 million years ago.

Many of these places are spiritually and culturally important for **Indigenous** peoples, including **Aboriginal** Australians and Torres Strait Islanders. Some natural sites are now protected areas because of their significance to Indigenous peoples.

Kandimalal, also known as Janyil or Wolfe Creek Crater, is a giant hollow in the ground made when a **meteorite** crashed into Earth. The crater is so large, it can be seen from space. The crash likely happened about 120,000 years ago. The site is important for Djaru and Walmajarri people, among others.

● Sturt Creek, Western Australia

Aboriginal people have many stories about Kandimalal. In one of the stories, the crater formed when a rainbow snake crawled out of the ground.

Large clusters of stromatolites can be found in the water in Australia.

Australia might have been the home of the earliest life on the planet. Material from Australian **stromatolites** was studied. It turned out to be the oldest known sign of life on Earth.

Slice of History

Australian National University student Steve Clement first designed and built the SHRIMP tool for analyzing rocks. SHRIMP stands for "sensitive high-resolution ion microprobe." It helps scientists understand more about early Earth and solar system history.

KANGAROOS AND A CORAL REEF

Australia is home to many unique plants and animals. You can swim among sea life in the Great Barrier Reef, the world's largest coral reef. Across the country, rainforest animals and ancient plants live in the Daintree region. Kangaroos, emus, and koalas are all famous Australian animals. But watch out for dangerous stonefish, funnel web spiders, and jack jumper ants! Researchers in Australia find new creatures all the time.

Rainforest

Opal

● Great Barrier Reef, Queensland

● Daintree National Park, Far North Queensland

● Lightning Ridge, New South Wales

● Australia Museum, Sydney, New South Wales

The Great Barrier Reef is a living thing on its own. The reef is made of the skeletons of an animal called coral.

Fossils give us clues about Australia's early history and living things. In the 1980s, Bob Foster found fossils while mining for a gemstone called opal in Lightning Ridge. He took them to scientists at the Australian Museum in Sydney, over 450 miles (almost 725 kilometers) away. In 2019, scientists confirmed that the fossils belonged to a new kind of dinosaur, which they named after Foster.

PROTECTING AUSTRALIA'S WILDLIFE

Scientists are working to protect Australia's natural life. Koalas eat mostly eucalyptus leaves, but eucalyptus forests are being burned to make more room for farmland. Rebecca Johnson, Katherine Belov, and a team of scientists recently discovered the **genetic** blueprint for koalas. Their efforts will help the koala's survival in Australia.

Rebecca Johnson is the first woman to become the director of the Australian Museum Research Institute.

Australian wildlife expert Steve Irwin worked with his wife, nature expert Terri Irwin, to teach others about the importance of wildlife. They turned Australia Zoo into a wildlife **conservation** center. Terri Irwin and their two children still own the zoo. They continue to promote conservation in Australia.

The Irwin family became famous around the world for their work in conservation.

Eucalyptus leaves can make many living things sick, but koalas can eat them with no problems.

Missing Tigers

It is thought that the last Tasmanian tiger, also called a thylacine, died in the late 1930s. But Australian scientist Andrew Pask and his team were able to make copies of the animal's genetic material. Among other things, they hope to discover why it looked and acted so much like a wolf.

NEW IDEAS FROM DOWN UNDER

Australian inventions have changed the world. Scientist and engineer Veena Sahajwalla invented a way to turn waste such as old phones into new materials. She also invented a process that uses old tires and plastics to make steel, a metal building material. This "green steel" is much better for the environment than the traditional kind.

Veena Sahajwalla

David Unaipon invented many things during his life, including special motors and wheels. One of his most famous inventions helps cut a sheep's wool without hurting the animal. His inventions and research earned him the nickname "the Australian Leonardo," after the famous Italian inventor.

David Unaipon

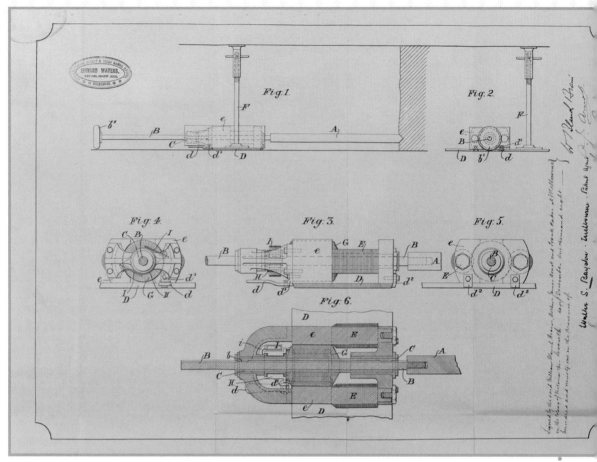

Arthur James Arnot and William Blanch Brain are credited with inventing the first electric drill.

The electric drill had its start in Melbourne, Victoria. It was developed in 1889 as a way to cut through rock to find oil and coal. Modern versions of this first drill are found in homes and businesses around the world.

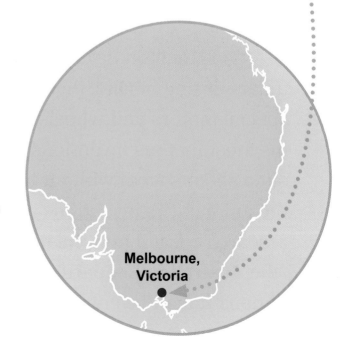

Melbourne,
Victoria

Life would hardly be the same without electric refrigerators, another Australian invention. The system to push gas through tubes to cool them was invented in the 1850s. The same idea is used to make refrigerators and air conditioners.

Many modern refrigerators still use a version of an Australian invention.

A Hot Record

Refrigerators and air conditioners are important in the high temperatures of Australia. On January 2, 1960, the hottest temperature in Australia was recorded. Oodnadatta, a town in South Australia, had a high temperature of 123 degrees Fahrenheit (about 50.6 degrees Celsius)!

INCREDIBLE BUILDINGS

The Sydney Opera House in Sydney, New South Wales, is one of the world's most famous buildings. It houses artistic performances from around the world. Its gigantic concrete shell shapes were a challenge for Australian engineers to design. The Opera House took 14 years to build.

Australian **architect** Glenn Murcutt has won many awards. His buildings are made for the high heat and winds common in Australia. He also makes sure that the materials can be found or made locally.

Murcutt designed this house with open sides and a high floor. These things let air flow through the house, cooling it.

Sydney Opera House

Sydney,
New South
Wales

Winning the Contest

A competition was held in Australia in 1956 for opera house designs. Danish architect Jørn Utzon sent in the winning entry. His design was used to create the Sydney Opera House.

Emily Kame Kngwarreye's art is so famous that it has been used on airplanes.

AUSSIE ART

Creative Australians produce amazing works of art. Emily Kame Kngwarreye is a famous Aboriginal painter. She painted in many different styles. Some of her paintings were inspired by things in nature, such as a plant called a bush yam.

Bronwyn Bancroft

Bronwyn Bancroft is a famous Bundjalung artist and writer. Her style is inspired by Aboriginal art that has been used for thousands of years. She works with groups to give training to young Aboriginal women in selling and creating art.

Aboriginal dot paintings are one of the most recognized styles of Australian art. Most traditional paintings are inspired by sacred rituals and ancient stories. At one point, art was the only written language on the continent. It was used to tell stories about beliefs, history, and survival skills.

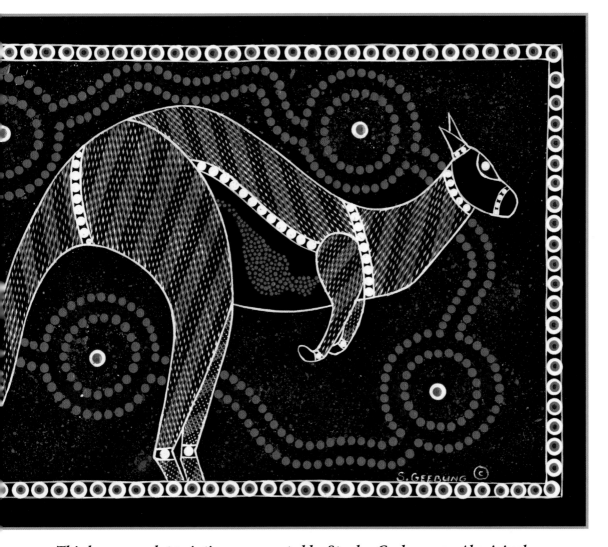

This kangaroo dot painting was created by Stanley Geebung, an Aboriginal artist. He is from the Gungarri people of Augathella in South West Queensland.

Movies would be very different without great Australian minds. The first full-length movie was made in Melbourne, Victoria, in 1906. It was more than 60 minutes long. Most movies of this kind were only ten minutes long then. Modern movies were changed by great Australians as well. Animal Logic in Crows Nest, Sydney, invented new ways to make movie special effects with computers. These effects are now used in many films. Animal Logic has won awards for their special effects in movies such as *Happy Feet*.

Animal Logic

First full-length movie

● Sydney, New South Wales

● Melbourne, Victoria

For some movie special effects, action is filmed on a green background. Special effects experts can then replace the green area with another background, such as one that looks like outer space.

The Story of the Kelly Gang

The first full-length feature film told the story of famous crimes by the Kelly Gang. The film was so popular that it was taken on tour through Australia, New Zealand, Ireland, and Great Britain.

SAFETY IN THE SKY

Airplane crashes interested Australian scientist David Warren. He invented the original flight recorder, called a black box. This machine records what happens to an **aircraft** while it is flying. If it crashes, the recorder can be used to get details about the crash. This can prevent more crashes in the future.

In 1965, Jack Grant invented an inflatable escape slide for aircraft. It makes it easier for people to leave a crashed plane safely. It can save many lives if there is a crash.

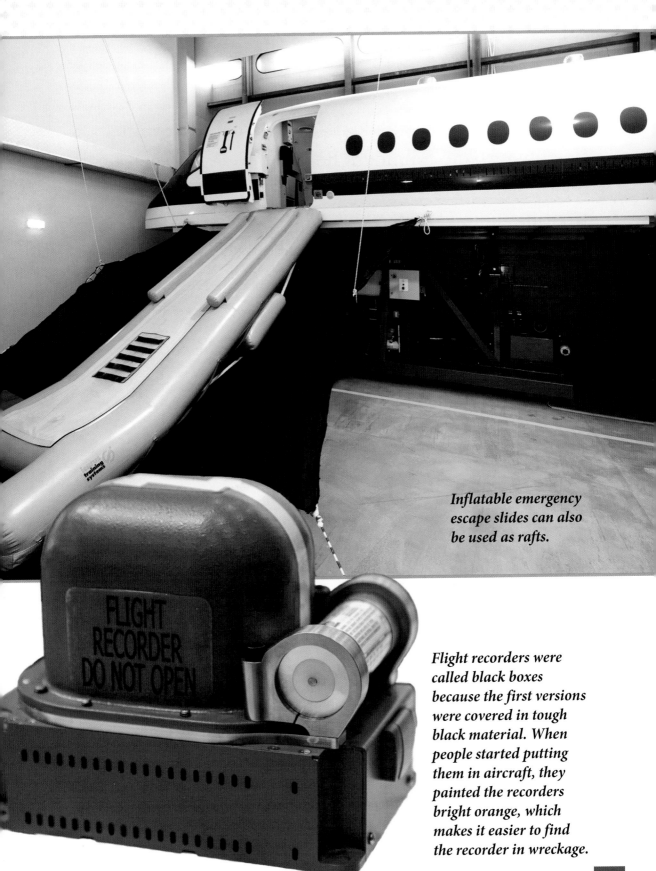

Inflatable emergency escape slides can also be used as rafts.

FLIGHT
RECORDER
DO NOT OPEN

Flight recorders were called black boxes because the first versions were covered in tough black material. When people started putting them in aircraft, they painted the recorders bright orange, which makes it easier to find the recorder in wreckage.

MEDICAL MARVELS

Australians have made many medical discoveries. Scientist Elaine Saunders helped develop special hearing aids. They can be adjusted by the person wearing them using an app. The batteries are also easy to change. Most hearing aids need a doctor's help to adjust them. She and the scientists at the Blamey Saunders lab are working on hearing aids that are even better and easier to use.

Hearing aids can sit inside of a person's ear. They make sounds such as talking louder. The louder sounds then travel into the person's ear so they can hear them.

Fiona Wood is famous for leading a team of doctors that saved 28 people after a bombing in Bali.

Australia is home to another incredible medical invention: spray-on skin. Professor Fiona Wood invented the technique to help people with burns. Skin cells are grown in a lab and sprayed onto the burned area. The patient can often grow skin faster and with less scarring after the treatment.

AWESOME AUSTRALIA

Australia and its people have brought the world many incredible discoveries and amazing ideas. How would your life be different without the great minds and finds of Australia? The more you learn about this remarkable continent, the more fascinating facts you will find.

Western Australia

Western Australia

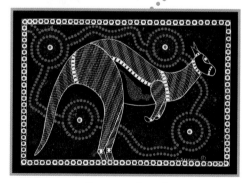
Queensland

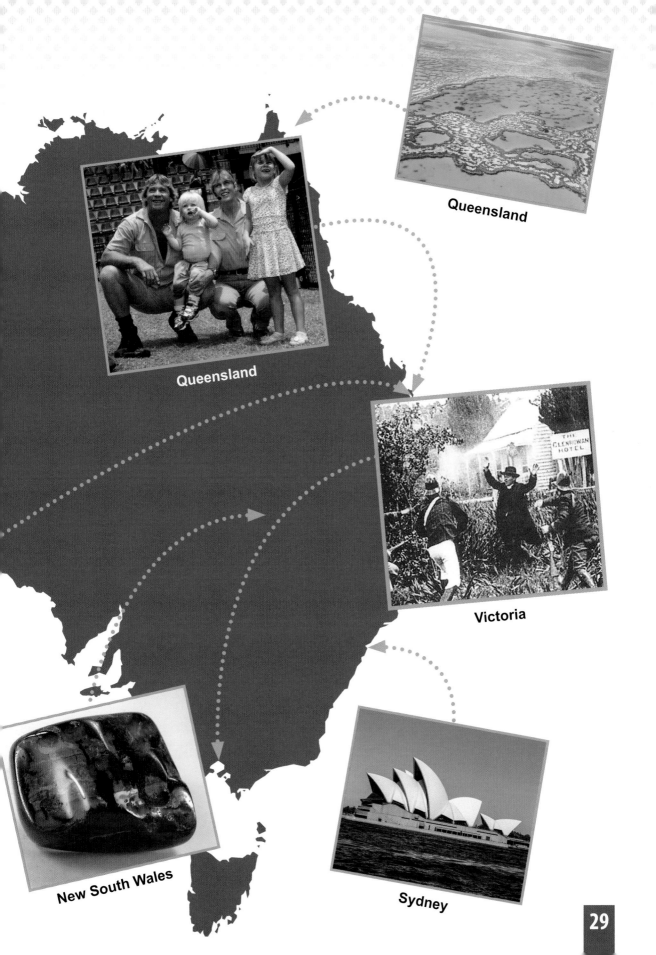

Queensland

Queensland

Victoria

New South Wales

Sydney

29

Glossary

Aboriginal (ab-uh-RIJ-uh-nuhl): one of the native peoples of Australia who have lived there since before the Europeans arrived

aircraft (AIR-kraft): a vehicle that can fly

architect (AHR-ki-tekt): someone who designs buildings and supervises the way they are built

conservation (kahn-sur-VAY-shuhn): the protection of valuable things, especially forests, wildlife, natural resources, or artistic or historic objects

genetic (juh-NET-ik): controlled by or having to do with genes and heredity

geological (jee-uh-LAH-ji-kuhl): related to Earth's physical structure, especially its layers of soil and rock

hemisphere (HEM-i-sfeer): one half of a round object, especially of Earth

Indigenous (in-DIJ-ehn-us): people living naturally or originally in a particular area

meteorite (MEE-tee-uh-rite): a piece of rock from space that fell to Earth

stromatolites (struh-MAT-uh-lytes): rocks with layers of bacteria and algae that are found in shallow saltwater environments

Index

Text-Dependent Questions

1. In what part of the continent do most Australians live?

2. What is Uluru?

3. Why is Australia a good place to study living things?

4. What did Fiona Wood invent?

5. How can black boxes make flying safer?

Extension Activity

Plan a tour through Australia to visit some of the places you read about in this book. Make a travel brochure to advertise the tour to others. What places will you include? Why did you include them?

About the Author

Robin Koontz is a freelance author and illustrator of a wide variety of nonfiction and fiction books, educational blogs, and magazine articles for children and young adults. Her 2011 science title *Leaps and Creeps: How Animals Move to Survive* was an Animal Behavior Society Outstanding Children's Book Award Finalist. Raised in Maryland and Alabama, Robin now lives with her husband in the Coast Range of western Oregon, where she especially enjoys observing the wildlife on her property. You can learn more on her blog at robinkoontz.wordpress.com.

www.rourkeeducationalmedia.com

PHOTO CREDITS: page 3: ©magann / iStockphoto.com; page 4: ©Puwadol Jaturawutthichai / Shutterstock.com;page 5: ©amophoto_au / shutterstock.com; page 5: ©Arunna / iStockphoto.com (binoculars); page 6: ©tiny-al / iStockphoto.com (top); page 6: ©simonbradfield / iStockphoto.com; page 7: ©Cezary Wojtkowski / iStockphoto.com; page 8: ©Terra > ASTER / NASA.gov (left); page 8: ©Stephan Ridgway / flckr.com; page 9: ©bennymarty / iStockphoto.com (top); page 9: ©Magnus Manske / Wikimedia; page 10: ©AustralianCamera / iStockphoto.com (top); page 10: ©RKBot / Wikimedia; page 11: ©mevans / iStockphoto.com; page 12: ©Nicholasjlangley / Wikimedia (top); page 12: ©Splash News / Newscom; page 13: ©Logorilla / iStockphoto.com (top); page 13: ©the_guitar_mann / iStockphoto.com; page 14: ©cihatatceken / iStockphoto.com (tires); page 14: ©DAVID GRAY/ REUTERS / Newscom; page 15: ©clickhere / iStockphoto.com; page 15: ©HappyWaldo / Wikimedia (David Unaipon); page 16: © / National Archives of Australia; page 17: ©phototropic / iStockphoto.com (top); page 17: ©ShannonND / Pixabay; page 18: ©ArquiWHAT / Wikimedia; page 19: ©Janette Zilioli / publicdomainpictures.net (top); page 19: ©W.Teodoro/Zeduce/Robert Wallace / Newscom; page 20: ©AEMoreira042281 / Wikimedia (top); page 20: ©Bronwynbancroft / Wikimedia; page 21: ©mollypix / iStockphoto.com; page 22: ©SeventyFour / Getty Images (top); page 22: ©Canicula / shutterstock.com; page 23: ©bjones27 / iStockphoto.com (top); page 23: ©Soerfm / Wikimedia; page 24: ©frankpeters / iStockphoto.com; page 25: ©Magnus Manske / Wikimedia (top); page 25: ©MB-one / Wikimedia; page 26: ©snapphoto / iStockphoto.com; page 27: ©Magnus Manske / Wikimedia; background: ©DavidZydd / Pixabay

Edited by: Tracie Santos
Cover and interior layout by: Book Buddy Media

Library of Congress PCN Data

Great Minds and Finds in Australia / Robin Koontz
(Discoveries Around the World)
ISBN 978-1-73163-799-4 (hard cover)(alk. paper)
ISBN 978-1-73163-876-2 (soft cover)
ISBN 978-1-73163-953-0 (e-Book)
ISBN 978-1-73164-030-7 (ePub)
Library of Congress Control Number: 2020930063

Rourke Educational Media
Printed in the United States of America
01-1942011937